LEARN EVERYDAY

WRITING SKILLS

By : Shradha Anand

DREAMLAND PUBLICATIONS
J-128, Kirti Nagar, New Delhi-110 015, India
Tel.: +91-11-2510 6050, 2543 5657
E-mail : dreamland@www.dreamlandpublications.com
Shop online at www.dreamlandpublications.com
Follow us on www.instagram.com/dreamland.publications

Published in 2025 by
DREAMLAND PUBLICATIONS
J-128, Kirti Nagar, New Delhi - 110 015, India
Tel : +91-11-2510 6050, 2543 5657
E-mail : dreamland@dreamlandpublications.com
www.dreamlandpublications.com

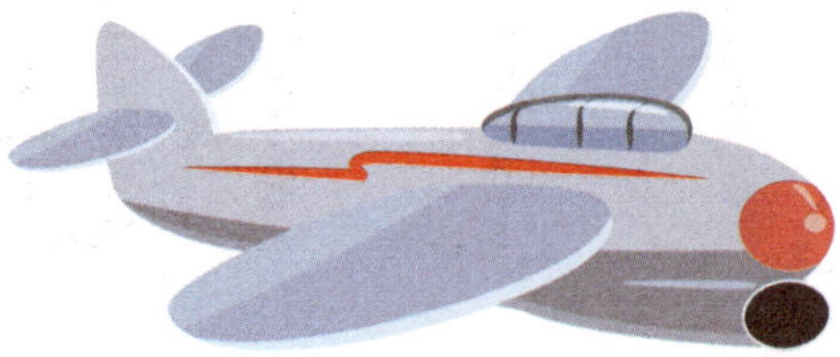

Preface

Activity books can be fun as well as educational for children. Children love activity books. There is so much to learn from these books. Keeping in mind the daily needs of all children, Dreamland Publications has endeavoured to come up with a series of 15 books 'Learn Everyday'. Each book of this series has a collection of activities that include simple math, writing, vocabulary, tracing, and more. Suitable for kids from preschoolers to first graders, each book of this series is a perfect activity book that is needed by the children to be successful.

Compound Words

Use each pair of pictures to make a compound word.

Paste the sticker of ball.

 +  = 

 +  =

 +  =

 +  =

 +  =

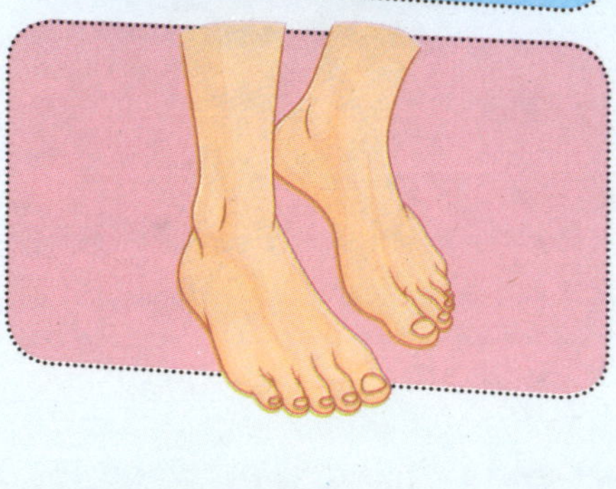 +  =

Story Writing

Rearrange the sentences in the correct order to form a story. Paste the sticker of fox.

The boy said, "I will take the fox. One day, a boy saw a fox sleeping on a hill. I will buy seeds with the money. I will sell its fur. I will get money. My seeds will become strong plants. People will want my plants. I will tell them to keep away from my plants. I will sow the seeds in the field. The people will not listen. The fox woke up. He jumped and ran away into the forest. The boy went away. I will shout at them." The boy called out loudly. KEEP AWAY.

H

A Birthday Bash

Choose the right words to complete the story.
Paste the stickers of balloons.

caps, toy, cake, game, pizza, balloons, friends, chairs, camera, gifts

It is my birthday. The room has many __________. There are __________ for sitting. My __________ have got me __________. Papa takes our picture with a __________. We wear colourful __________. We play the tail the donkey __________. Susie wins the game and gets a __________ as a prize. There is a yummy __________ to cut and __________ to eat. Let us enjoy.

The Cat and the Mouse

Read the story and make polite sentences as given.
Then complete the story. Paste the stickers.

Once there was a cat and a mouse.
They lived in the same house.
One day, the cat bit off the mouse's tail.
Mouse: Cat, please return my tail.
Cat: No, first bring me some milk.
The mouse went to the cow.
Mouse: Cow, please give me some milk for the cat.
Cow: First, bring me some hay.

The mouse went to the farmer.

Mouse: Farmer, ____________________

Farmer: First, bring me some meat.

The mouse went to the butcher.

Mouse: Butcher, ____________________.

Butcher: First, bring me some bread.

The mouse went to the baker.

Mouse: Baker, ____________________

Baker: Here is some bread.

The mouse took the bread to the ______________.

The butcher gave the mouse ________________.

The mouse took the meat to the ______________

The farmer gave the mouse ________________

The mouse took the hay to ________________.

The cow gave the mouse ________________

The mouse took the milk to ________________

The cat gave the mouse, its ________________.

When I Grow Up

Fill in the blanks to tell who you are when you grow up.
Paste the stickers.

I will wear a ____________ colour of uniform.

My shirt will be ____________.

My pants will be____________.

I might wear a _____________ helmet or cap.

I will carry a _________________.

My shoes will be ___________________.

I will be a ____.

Feelings

Write the feeling that you feel. Use the box. Paste the stickers.

happy, sad, angry, upset, nervous, bored

I am ________________.
I lost my favourite pencil.

I am ________________.
I did not study well for the test.

I am ________________.
I just received a present.

I am ________________.
My friend fought with me.

I am ________________.
My friend tore my book.

I am ______________.
I have no one to play with.

Blend It

Write a quick word with the given blends in each row. Then use the words in each row to make a sentence and paste the stickers.

	fl	tr	gr	fr
	pl	gr	gl	pr
	br	cl	sr	cr
	sn	tr	sl	pl
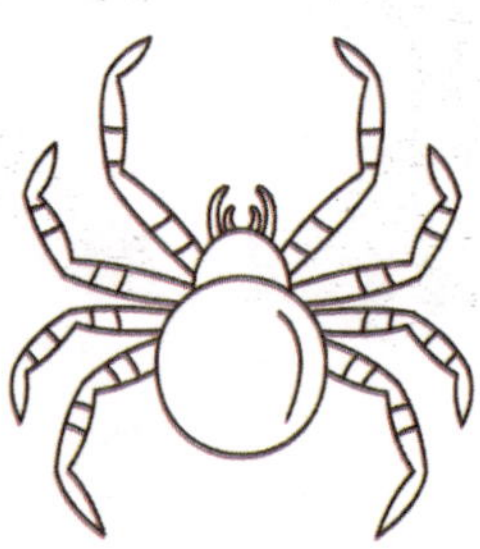	cr	br	sp	pr

Yes or No

**Look at the pictures and write down yes or no.
Paste the sticker of cat.**

The fish is ugly.

The car is new.

The monkey is thin.

The cat is sad.

The giraffe is short.

The bag is heavy.

The train is long.

What is the word?

Look at the pictures for clues and write the correct word.

1 The ______ carried the corn to the hill. (aunt/ant)

2 The dog has thick coat of ______. (fir/fur)

3 I can see a ______ in the closed coop. (foul/fowl)

4 The car applied the ______ at the crossing. (break/ brake)

5 This ______ has long horns. (dear/deer)

6 The horse's ______ is short to hold. (rain/rein)

7 I like to eat a large ______ from my plate. (bury/berry)

8 Sit on the lower ______ in the train. (birth/berth)

Stretch the Sentence

Rewrite the sentences by adding words and stretching it.

1. I saw a snake under the rock.

2. My brother ate a sandwich.

3. The girl cleaned.

4. Mother is going for shopping.

5. I heard the dog.

6. The quilt is on the bed.

Mike at the Farm

Read the story and answer.

The cow drinks from the tub.
I drink some milk.

The cat runs after a rat.
The hen lays an egg for me.

The goat eats grass.
The sheep gives wool for my cap.

The dog plays in the mud.
I play with him too.

We enjoy at the farm. We sing and eat. We play a lot.

Write the answer.

1. Where is Mike? ______
2. Who eats grass? ______
3. Who lays egg? ______
4. Who play in mud? ______

Who runs after rat? ______

My Happiest Day

Remember your happiest day. Answer these questions. Paste the stickers.

1. Why were you happy?

2. When were you happy?

3. Who made you happy?

4. Where were you when you were happy?

5. How did you feel inside to be happy?

6. How did you show that you are happy?

7. What did you say in happiness?

8. What did you do in happiness?

My Last Sunday

Write down about last Sunday. Paste the sticker.

Where I went?

Who I saw?

What I ate?

What I played?

Who came home?

What I wanted to do?

What was fun?

My Things

Look at the pictures and form sentences. Paste a sticker.

Car Clubs

Suppose you are at the playground playing a sport with your friends. Use these words to write a paragraph.

then before earlier first third finally
next after second last later

At the Zoo

Paste the sticker of cat.

What have you seen at the zoo that is:

Red		Fluffy	
Black		Tiny	
Orange		Huge	
Yellow		Furry	
Brown		Friendly	
White		Growling	
		Sleepy	
		Hungry	

The Carrot Soup

Read the story and answer in one word. Paste the stickers.

My name is Tom. I live in a red house. My father and mother live with me. My grandfather and grandmother also live with me. I have a little sister too. We play with her doll and my ball. My grandfather has a garden. He grows vegetables in the garden. His little carrot has grown big. He wants grandma to make soup with the carrot. He cannot pull it out. We all help grandfather to pull the carrot out of the soil. We pull and pull. The carrot comes out a little. We pull more and more. The carrot comes out a little more. We pull a lot. The carrot comes out. We clap happily. We all drink carrot soup.

1. What is the colour of Tom's house? ________
2. Who is little in his house? ________
3. Where does the carrot grow? ________
4. What does grandmother make? ________
5. Where does the carrot grow? ________

Birthday Invitation

Complete the birthday invitation. Paste the stickers.

Dear ________________,

My birthday is on ____________. I will be ______ years old.

Please come for the party to _____________.

I have called ___________ and ____________ also.

We will eat _____________ and _________________.

We will play _____________ and ________________.

The party will begin at _________________.

Your friend,

____

Action Time

Read and do the action. Write the name of each body part. Paste the sticker of ear.

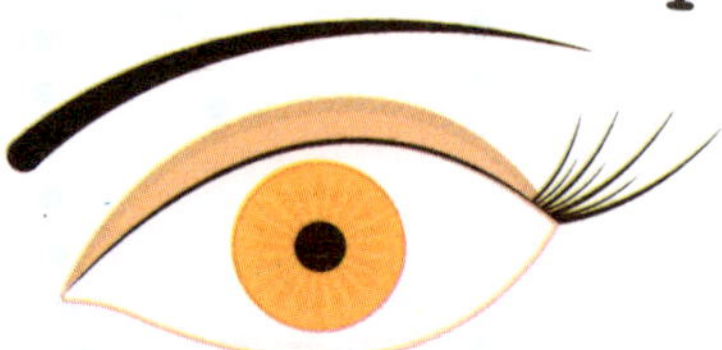

turn your head to the left
bend your knees
wave your arms
blink you eyes
shrug your shoulders
touch your toes
clap your hands
pull your ears

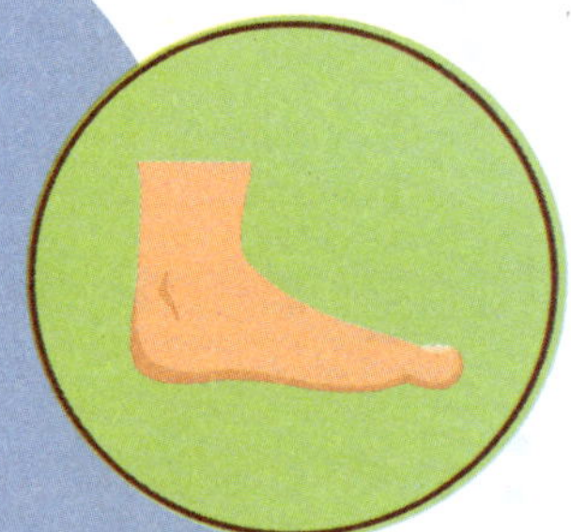

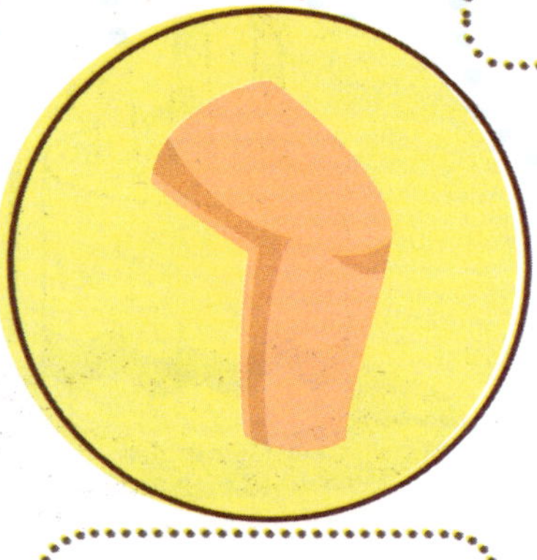

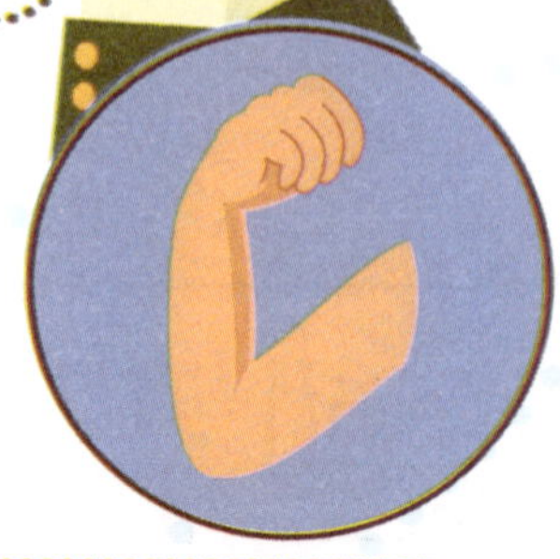

Grandpa and Grandma

Read the description of Grandpa.

1. My grandpa is tall.
2. His hands are large.
3. He wears glasses.
4. He has grey hair.
5. He likes noodles.
6. He helps me to learn to swim.
7. He drives a fancy blue car.

Now write the description of your grandma.

....

....

....

....

....

....

....

Minty Rabbit wants a House

Read Minty Rabbit's Story and tick the correct words. Paste the sticker.

Minty is a rabbit. He looks for a house.

Lion: You can live in my den, Minty.

Minty: No, your den is dark and big.

Fish: You can live in my pond, Minty.

Minty: I cannot swim. I will get wet.

1. Lion lives in	den	coop.
2. Minty cannot	fly	hop.
3. Minty will get wet in the	hole	pond.
4. Minty lives with	fish	mole.
5. Mole lives in a	nest	hole.

Double Letters

Can you write the double letters and make words?

ra___ ___it

b___ ___t

do___ ___

r___ ___d

bu___ ___on

h___ ___f

ki___ ___en

sci___ ___ors

be___ ___y

pu___ ___et

b___ ___t

bu___ ___

gu___ ___

h___ ___l

h___ ___p

What Can You Do?

Circle the correct words. Paste the sticker of tiger.

Fish – I can skip /swim.

Tiger- I can sprint/fly.

Bird: I can hop /flutter.

Rabbit – I can hop/crawl.

Monkey – I can climb/roar.

Horse – I can bleat/gallop.

Tell a Friend

Answer for yourself with a tick or a cross.

Can you plant a seed?

....

Can you cook?

....

Can you dance?

....

Can you swim?

....

Can you catch a ball?

....

Can you drive a scooter?

....

Can you read a story?

....

Can you run fast?

....

Can you draw an animal?

....

A Naughty Rabbit

Complete this story using picture words.

Four little __________  lived under a very big fir ________ 

One day, old Mrs Rabbit took her ____________ 

and _______________  and went to baker.

The four little rabbits hopped down the ___________  to pick

_____________  Peter was naughty. He ran to farmer's

_________________ . He went under the______. 

He ate lettuce, and ____________   Next, he ate the

__________.  Farmer ran after him. Peter ran

around and lost both his__________.  His ____________

 got caught in the__________. 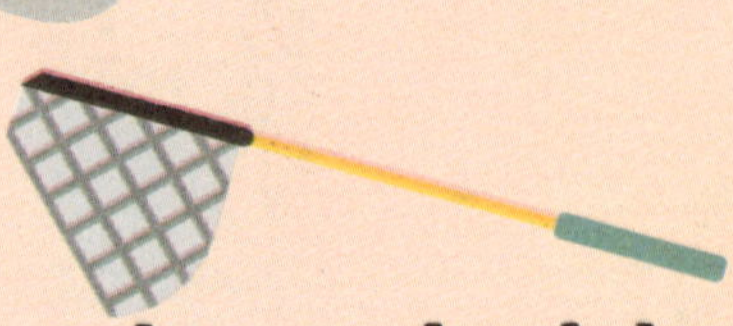

He hid in a __________  of water. Later he ran back home.

Dinosaurs

Fill in the blanks with location words. Paste the sticker.

on, in, behind, in front of, between

1. The red dinosaur is ______ the helicopter.
2. The green dinosaur is ______ the cycle.
3. The yellow dinosaur is __________ the red and the green dinosaur.
4. The green dinosaur is ___________ the yellow dinosaur.
5. The red dinosaur is _________ the yellow dinosaur.

Market Visit

Read the story and complete the sentences.

Nancy and Mummy go to the market by car. She loves fruits. On the way, she waves at Dr Pat outside the hospital. She sees the zoo and the park. Her mummy takes gas from the gas station. They stop at the old bank to take out some money. Soon they reach the market. The market has a big fruit shop. There are red apples and yellow mangoes. There are green grapes and orange oranges too! Nancy's mummy buys mangoes. Nancy will eat mangoes with her grandma. Nancy's mummy takes oranges to make fresh juice. She also takes a bunch of fresh and juicy grapes. The fruit seller puts all the fruits in a little bag. Nancy is very happy.

1. Nancy loves to eat ____________.
2. Nancy goes with her mother in the ________ to the _________.
3. She sees ________ and _______ on the way.
4. Her mother takes gas at the ______________.
5. The apples are ________ and mangoes are ________.
6. Nancy's grandma also likes ____________.
7. Mother will make juice from the _________.
8. Nancy is __________ at the end.

With a Neighbour

Talk to a neighbour and write down here. Paste the stickers.

1. What is your full name?

2. Where were your born?

3. How old are you?

4. What work do you do?

5. What is the colour of your vehicle?

6. Where is your office?

7. How many years have you lived here?

Silent Letters

Look at the pictures and their names. Write the silent letters in the given circles.

Lamb

Castle

Ghost

Knee

Sword

Gnome

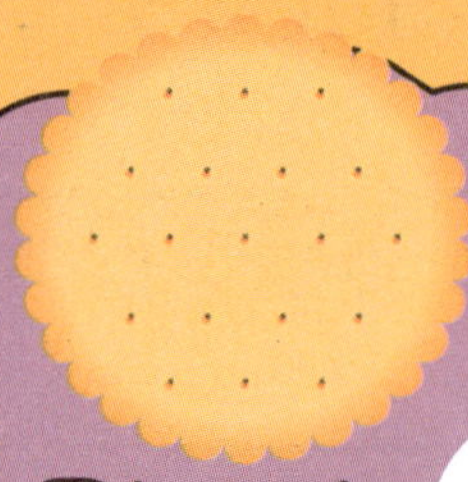

Biscuit

Salmon

Raspberry

Island

Bridge

Sandwich

Write a story using all the words given above.

Robby's First day to School

It is Robby's first day at school. His papa gives him a book. His mother gives him a lunch box. Robby will share his lunch. His grandfather gives him a water bottle. Robby will drink water. His grandmother gives him a pencil box. Robby has a pencil, an eraser, and crayons. He will write and colour. Robby packs his things in his school bag. He wears his bag on his shoulder. Beep, Beep. He hears the school bus. He quickly goes outside the house. The school bus has come. Robby sits inside the bus and goes to school. When Robby reaches school he sees that he has forgotten to get his water bottle. Robby is sad. Now, what will he do? "Robby, Robby," calls a voice. Robby looks behind him. It is his grandfather. He is in his yellow car. He has got Robby's water bottle. Robby runs to him and takes his bottle. "Thank you, grandpa."

1. What does Robby pack in his school bag?

____

2. Who help him?

____

3. How does Robby go to school?

____

4. What does he forget at home?

____

5. Why does Robby thank Grandpa in the end?

____

Riddle Time

Read the riddle and name each object.

It is long and has a black end. You write with it.

It is small. You use it to rub mistakes.

It is long and thin. You use it to draw a line.

It is small. It is colourful. You use it to make a picture.

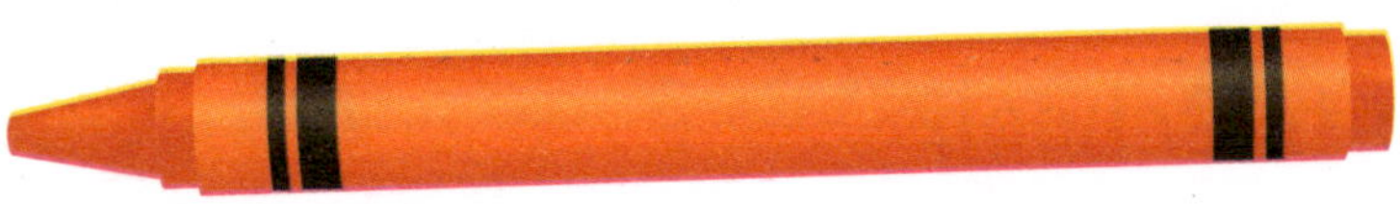

It is square and thick. It has many pages.

Vehicles

Write the words that complete each sentence.

1. A train runs on t____________.
2. I like to go by the school v____________.
3. Mother rides a s______________.
4. I have a little green b ______________.
5. Father and I went in a big a_____________ to America.

Identify each vehicle and count them.

It is small and has an engine and a boot. It has four wheels.

____

It is big and has many wheels. It runs on the road.

____

It sails in the water. It has oars.

____

It flies in the sky. It has wings.

____

Picture Play

Look at the picture and answer the questions. Paste the sticker.

1. Where are all the animals?

____

2. What is in the middle of the ground?

____

3. What is the bear doing?

____

4. How's the weather?

____

5. Are the animals looking happy? Yes or no.

____

6. Who is leaning over the bear?

____

The Elephant and the Tailor

Read the story and answer the questions.

Once, an elephant got in friendship with a tailor. The elephant used to go to a river for a bath daily and pass by a tailor's shop. The tailor would give it something to eat. One day the tailor was in an angry mood due to a quarrel. The elephant came. Instead of giving anything to eat, the tailor pricked the elephant's trunk with his needle. The elephant felt pain. He went to the river, had his bath, and then filled up its trunk with muddy water. He stopped at the tailor's shop and threw muddy water on the garments in the shop. The clothes were spoilt. The tailor suffered a great loss. He felt sad. But it was too late.

1. Why does the elephant go to the river?

____

2. What does tailor do with the elephant while in angry mood?

____

3. What does the elephant fill his trunk with?

____

4. Why does the tailor suffer a great loss?

____

5. How does the tailor feel in the end?

____

The Camel

Read about the camel and write true or false.

You must have seen a camel. It is a very useful domestic animal. It does a number of jobs for its master. It gives rides and carries loads on its back. It draws loaded carts and ploughs, as well. The camel is useful in deserts where food and water are limited. It can cover long journeys in the hot sand. It has padded feet that do not sink in the sand. So the camels can run fast in the sand very easily. That is why the camel is called—Ship of the Desert.

1. Camel is a domestic animal. __________
2. It cannot do many jobs. __________
3. It draws loaded carts and ploughs as well. __________
4. Deserts have lots of water. __________
5. Camel has soft feet. __________

A Newspaper

Read and answer the questions. Paste the sticker.

I am a newspaper. I was printed in a printing press. Then I was sent to a store. The storekeeper had many newspapers. I am written in English. I have many pages. I met newspapers written in many other languages. The shopkeeper sent me to a house in the morning. Everyone was waiting for me. Grandpa read the news on sports sipping his tea. Father read the news about the neighbourhood. Mother read about a dress sale in me. She told grandma about it. Kia, the little girl came to see the big pictures in me. Father made her read some sentences from me. Then she went to school. I was very happy that everyone had used me and read me.

1. Where is a newspaper made?

____

2. How does mother use it?

____

3. How does father use it?

____

4. How does Kia use it?

____

5. What does it have?

____

Note Writing

Shiny wrote a note to her grandfather. Write a similar note to your uncle thanking him for the gift he sent to you. Paste the sticker.

Dear Grandpa

I really like the dress that you bought for me.
I will wear it to school on my birthday.
Thank you very much.

Your granddaughter
Nancy

A Telephone

Read the paragraph and answer the following questions.

My phone is very smart. I can play a game on it. I can take a photo too. I can share it with everyone and you. Mum can find an address in it. Dad can send an email to the boss. Grandpa can play some music. One day grandma had to send a message I got my phone for her to send one. She said a thank you to me and gave me a warm brown bun!

1. What can the phone do with a click?

____

2. What does mum use the phone for?

____

3. How does it help grandma?

____

4. Who listens to music on it?

____

5. What did grandma give me?

____

School Carnival

Read the story of a lovely school carnival and fill in the blanks. Paste the sticker of boy.

Ryan went to the school carnival today. He had a lot of fun. He took a ride on the toy train. He ate ice cream and drank lemonade. He played a game and got a toy bear as a prize. He decided to gift it to his little sister. Ryan also sat for a magic show. The magician took out a coin from inside his ear. When the carnival was over Ryan thanked the teachers and said goodbye to his friends. He went home and told his grandparents all about the fun he had at the carnival.

Ryan went to the ______________.

He told his ______________ about it.

He thanks the ______________.

He won a ______________.

He gave the prize to his ______________.

The ____________ took out a __________ from his ear.

He drank ________________.

He took a ride on toy ________________.

The Banana

Read the funny story about a little monkey.
Correct the sentences and rewrite.

Little Monkey did not like to eat bananas. His parents were worried as he wanted ice cream all day. One day, grandmother monkey visited them. The father and mother monkey told her the matter. She made a suggestion. She told the father and mother monkey to put bananas in the ice cream. So they climbed the tree and got bananas. Little Monkey loved the new taste of ice cream. When they told him the secret he was surprised. He asked to eat a banana. Little monkey loves bananas now. Everyone is happy.

1. Little monkey loves apples.

____

2. One day, grandfather monkey paid a visit.

____

3. Father and mother monkey got pears from the tree.

____

4. Little monkey liked the taste of the cake.

____

5. He wanted to eat watermelon.

____

Picnic in the Garden

Read about a lovely picnic and tick the right word.

It is a sunny Sunday. Mother says that there is going to be a picnic in the park. Pat runs to get his ball. Joey brings a stick to play with Spot, the dog. Father puts some food and drink in the picnic basket. Mother carries a rug and they all go into the garden. Mother spreads the rug under the tree. She has a nice book to read. Father switches the radio on. There is music playing. Pat plays with his ball. He throws it around. Joey throws the stick far and Spot looks at him. He wants to play with the ball. He does not want to fetch the stick. Everyone laughs. Mother serves lemonade and apple slices. What a lovely picnic.

The picnic day is	Saturday	Sunday
Pat takes to picnic his	doll	ball
Mother brings a	rug	bug
The book is read by	father	mother
Spot wants to play with	stick	ball
They all drink	juice	lemonade

Snails

Read about snails and write true or false. Paste the stickers.

Snails are one of the oldest animals on the planet. Giant African land snail is the largest snail on the planet. The snails can be bright yellow, orange, or red. They can also be white, grey, or brown. Snails have a strong, muscular foot and coiled shell. Snail uses the shell as shelter. Snail has two pairs of tentacles on its head. Eyes are located on top of the long tentacles. Snail is active at night. Snails don't have teeth. Snails are the slowest animals on the planet. These animals can be kept as pets. Would you like a snail as a pet?

Snails are one of the oldest animals on the planet. ______

Giant African land snail is the smallest snail. ______

Snail has coiled shell. ______

Snail has four pairs of tentacles on its head. ______

Eyes are located on top of the long tentacles. ______

Snail is active during day. ______

Snails have sharp teeth. ______

Snails are the slowest animals. ______

The Earth Day

Pattie and Kenny are brother and sister. Find out what they do on Earth Day and write the words. Paste the sticker.

Pattie and Kenny love the garden. They help their mother in the garden and plant flower seeds.

Pattie loves her house. She goes around the house and turns off the lights and water of the leaking tap.

Kenny loves his red bike. He does not use the hose to clean it. Kenny cleans his bicycle with a wet mop.

Pattie and Kenny like animals. They go to the backyard and feed the animals. The birds come to play in their birdbath. They leave cut fruit for the rabbit and acorns for the squirrel.

Pattie likes to go shopping. She goes to buy recycled paper to cover her storybook. Kenny goes to bring a new glass bottle to take to school.

In the evening, Pattie and Kennie go with grandfather to clean the park. They carry a garbage bag and collect all the litter throw in the park.

Pattie turns off the water of the leaking ____________.

They leave ________________ for the squirrel.

They carry a __________________ to the park.

Pattie covers her storybook with __________________.

Kenny will take a ____________ water bottle to school.

Kenny has a ___________ ________ to clean his red bicycle.

They help their _________________ in the garden.

Jennie's Umbrella

Read about Jennie's umbrella and write the words for the pictures.

Jennie has a pretty yellow umbrella. Her mother gave it to her on her birthday. Jennie keeps it carefully in the rack. She carries it when it is very sunny outside. She carries it when it is raining outdoors. Jennie takes it to school and to the park. One day, Jenny lost her umbrella. She had taken it to the park and forgot it on the bench there. Jenny was crying a lot at home when there was a ring of the bell. It was the guard from the park. He had got back the umbrella. Jenny thanked him. The guard told her, "You are a good little girl and always politely greet me. I know you love your yellow umbrella. Keep it carefully."

____

____

____

____

____

My Cool Dad

Read about cool dad and match the columns.

My dad is very cool. He wears a striped shirt and polka dot shorts. He carries the beach ball and goes in his car to the beach. He plays beach ball with his friends. He is very strong. He rows a boat till the cliff. He brings flowers for me from there. Dad carries a sandwich in his pouch. Mum knows he likes tuna sandwiches. He sits on the wet sand and eats it. Dad never litters. He always leaves the beautiful beach clean and rides back home. Yes, my dad is very cool.

Column A	Column B
Striped	Friend
Polka Dot	Boat
Beach	Shorts
Sandwich	Flowers
Cliff	Ball
Car	Pouch
Play	Ride
Row	Shirt

Polar Bears

Read about polar bears. Find the correct spelling from the paragraph for the given words. Paste the sticker of seal.

Polar bears live in Russia, Alaska, Canada, Greenland, and Norway. They are large in size. They have transparent fur. Polar bears have a thick layer of blubber which keeps them warm. They like to run and swim. Polar bears spend most of their time in the water, where they hunt seals. Polar bears break chunks of ice, kick snow, or growl when they are angry. Polar bears live 15-18 years in the wild.

Poler

Beer

Rushia

Caneda

Larg

Transparant

Blabber

Seel

Chunc

Graowl

Angree

I can do Myself

Read about what I can do and write down six things that you can do! Paste the sticker.

I am seven years now. I can do many things myself. I can set the alarm clock at night. I get up on time to go to school. I can eat my food with a fork and spoon without a spill. I can button my shirt and tie my shoelaces. I can even swim to the deep side of the pool with dad. I can carry the heavy bag for my old neighbour. I can help little Ben skip rope. I can read a book and spell words. I can play many games and bounce the ball. I am a big boy now and I can do so many things.

Mia likes English

Read about Mia's favourite subject at school. Rewrite about your favourite subject like Mia.

Mia loves English. She has a thick English book. It has many stories and poems. Mia can tell about the pictures in her book. She can sing two poems from it. Mia's teacher teaches her new English words. Mia's mother teaches her to read well. Mia's father checks her if she makes a mistake. Mia is very smart now because she likes English. Mia keeps a bookmark inside her book. She has covered it with green paper. Mia keeps her book in her bag. She reads it at night. Tonight, she is reading a poem.

....

....

....

....

....

....

....

....

Making a Sandwich

Read the story and number the steps to tell how Victor makes a sandwich.

Victor's mother is not well. She is sick. Victor is making his sandwich for school himself. He has seen his mother do it for him many times. He takes two slices of bread. He cuts the edges. Victor spreads butter on one slice. He spreads cheese on the other slice. Victor cuts a tomato and puts on one slice. He sprinkles salt and pepper on it. He covers it with the other slice. Then Victor cuts two triangles. He has two sandwiches. He puts one into his lunch box. He goes and serves the other one to his sick mother. Victor is a good boy!

Boy puts butter on one slice.

Boy cuts the edges of bread slices.

Boy puts tomato on one slice.

Boy spreads cheese on the other slice.

Boy sprinkles salt and pepper.

Boy covers it with other slice.

Boy cuts two triangles.

Boy serves one slice to his sick mother.

Clown Fish

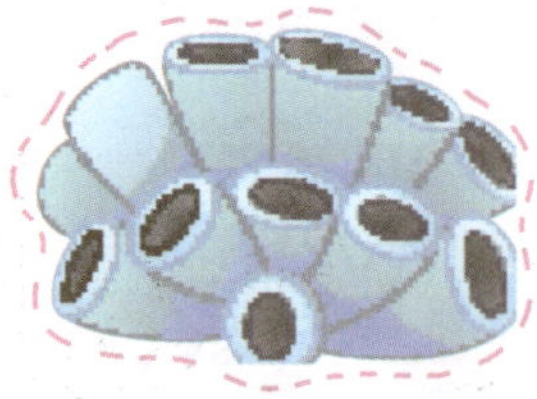

Read and label the picture with the correct words. Paste the sticker.

Clownfish is a small fish. It lives in the Indian and Pacific oceans, the Red Sea, and the Australian Great Barrier Reef. Clownfish live in the warm water, near the coral reefs. Clownfish are small in size. Clownfish are covered with white stripes that are combined with the orange, red, yellow, blue, or black basic colour of the body. Clownfish eat anemone's leftovers that are pieces of fish. Clownfish also eat algae and plankton. Do you want to know what this is? Clownfish are often kept as pets.

clownfish, Australian Barrier Reef, ocean, sea anemone, algae

Pia on the Bus

Read about Pia and answer the questions.
Paste the sticker of boy.

Pia takes a bus to go around her neighbourhood. She goes by bus to school. She stands in a queue to wait for the bus. She gets into the bus and sits by the window. Pia never puts her head or hand out of the window. She sits quietly. She sees that the bus stops at the traffic signal if it is red. She sees it move when the signal is green. Often Pia goes to the market by bus too. Her mother goes with her. They stand in the bus and let the old people have a seat.

1. How does Pia go around the neighbourhood?

____

2. How does she wait for the bus?

____

3. Where does she sit in the bus?

____

4. What does the bus do when the traffic signal is red?

____

5. Where else does Pia go by bus?

____

An Apple

Read about apples and fill in the blanks. Paste a sticker.

An apple is such a crunchy fruit. It is red, green and even yellow. Apples are sweet and sour too. They are juicy and very easy to carry to school. Mother always buys apples when she goes to the market. She makes apple pudding and apple pie for me. She sprinkles salt or sugar on apple slices and gives them to grandma. Mother has collected apple seeds. This year we will sow the seeds to grow our own apple tree. She says that apples grow in cold places on short trees.

Name of fruit			
Colour			
Taste			
Dishes made from it			
Where they grow			

T-Rex

Read about T-Rex. Choose the right dinosaur picture based on your reading. Paste the sticker of dinosaur.

The name 'Tyrannosaurus' means 'king of the tyrant lizards'. 'Tyranno' is the Greek word for tyrant, 'Saurus' is the Greek word for lizard, and 'Rex' is the Latin word for king. T-Rex was a large dinosaur that lived in western North America. His skull alone could reach a length of 5 feet. His small arms made it to catch prey. The T-Rex walked on two legs and was able to balance his head with his long, heavy tail.

Tails

Read about tails and match the animals to their tails.

Animals have tails. A cow has a thin tail to swish and drive away mosquitoes and flies. A fox has a bushy tail to show off. A dog has a curled long tail. A cat's tail stands erect when it is angry or in danger. Have you seen the tail of an elephant? It is very thin and long. Do you like the silken tail of a horse? It looks grand. Well, a rabbit has a small tail called a stump. Look behind you. You don't have a tail!

Cactus

Read about cactus and label their shapes. Paste a sticker.

Cactus is a type of plant that can store large amounts of water and survive in the desert. Cactus can have tree-like, cylindrical, rounded, irregular, or starfish shape. Cacti can be green, bluish, or brown-green in colour. They have a waxy surface. Cacti have spines instead of leaves. Spines can be soft or rigid, straight or curved, arranged in rows, or scattered. Since cacti live in dry areas, they need to absorb a large amount of water and store it in the stem and roots. The size and shape of the flower can be white, red, orange, pink, or blue in colour. Cacti can live for even 300 years.

Pumpkin Pumpkin!

Enjoy reading about the pumpkin and write about your favourite fruit or vegetable like this.

The name "pumpkin" originates from the Greek word "pepon", which means "large melon". Pumpkin is a fruit. Pumpkin grows on a vine. It produces oval or round fruit. It can be green, yellow, white, or red fruit. Its leaves are large and dark green in colour. Pumpkin flowers are yellowish-orange in colour and shaped like trumpets Pumpkin is a rich source of vitamins. Pumpkin can be consumed in the form of various sweet and salty dishes. Pumpkin pie is traditionally eaten on Thanksgiving Day. Pumpkin is also used as food for animals.

Going for a Movie

Read the story. Find five words from the story and circle in the movie reel.

MOVIETICKETPOPCORNINTERVALSLUSH

Penny is going to watch a movie with her class at school. She has given the money for her movie ticket to her teacher. All the children are excited. They are carrying small water bottles. Penny and her friends board the school bus. They arrive at the movie theatre. The teacher makes them form a queue. The children get a ticket from the box office and they enter the movie hall. The movie is a lot of fun. They watch it. At the interval, they go and get popcorn and slush. Penny shares her cheese popcorn with her friends. After the movie is over, the children get back on the bus. They discuss the movie. They have to write and draw what they saw for a class project.

My Missing Doll

Read about Jolly and answer the questions. Paste a sticker.

Jolly wants to play with her doll. But where is it? She cannot find it. Her mum tells her to go look for it around the house. Jolly goes to the living room and looks under the couch. She does not find her doll. But she finds her slippers. Jolly looks for it under the rug. Her doll is not there but her pink clip is there. Jolly goes to her bedroom. She looks at her slippers and her pink clip. She drops on the bed. She feels something hard under her pillow. It is her doll! Jolly found her doll, slippers, and her pink clip.

What does Jolly want to play with? ________

Who tells her to search for it? ________

What is under the couch? ________

What is under the rug? ________

Where is the doll? ________

ANSWERS

Page-3

Page-4

Page-5

Page-6

Page-7

Page-8

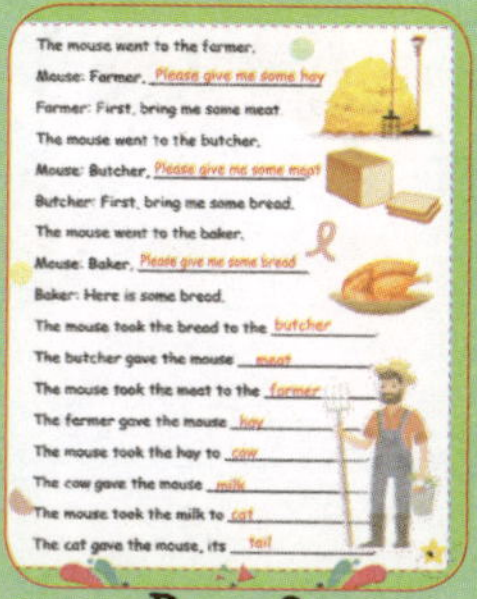
Page-9

Page-10

Page-11

Page-12

Page-13

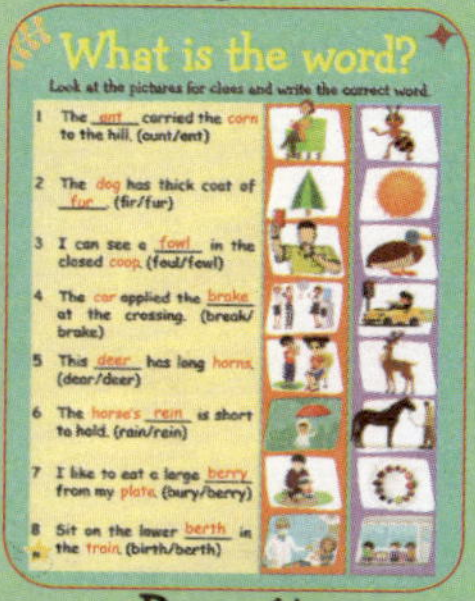

Page-14

Page-15

Page-16

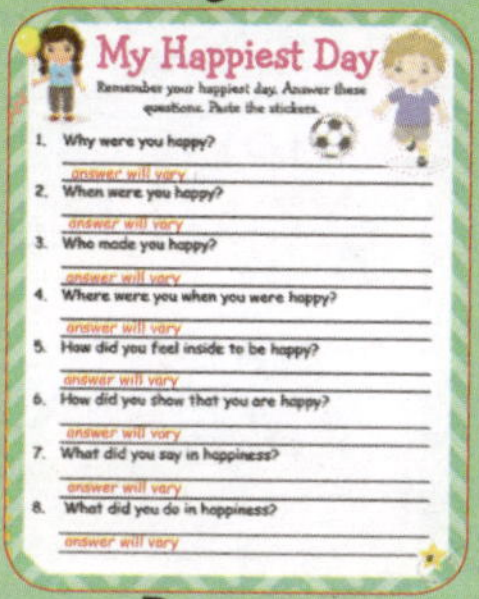

Page-17

Page-18

Page-19

Page-20

Page-21

Page-22

Page-23

Page-24

Page-25

Page-26

Page-27

Page-28

Page-29

Page-30

Page-31

Page-32

Page-33

Page-34

Page-35

Page-36

Page-37

Page-38

ANSWERS

Page-39

Page-40

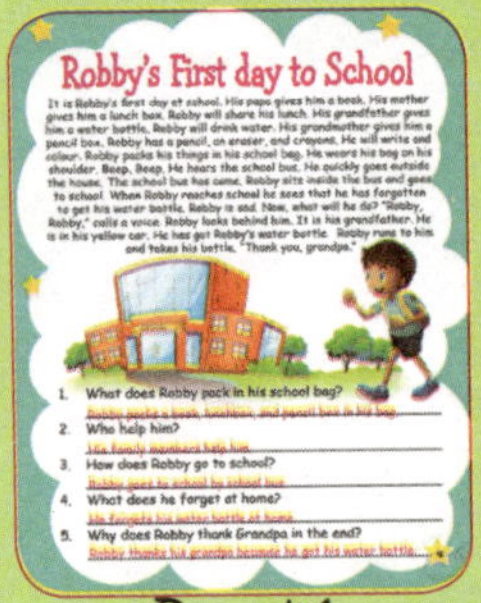
Page-41

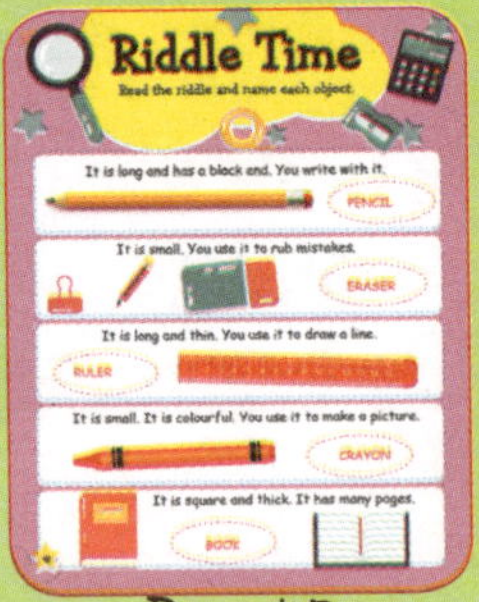
Page-42

Page-43

Page-44

Page-45

Page-46

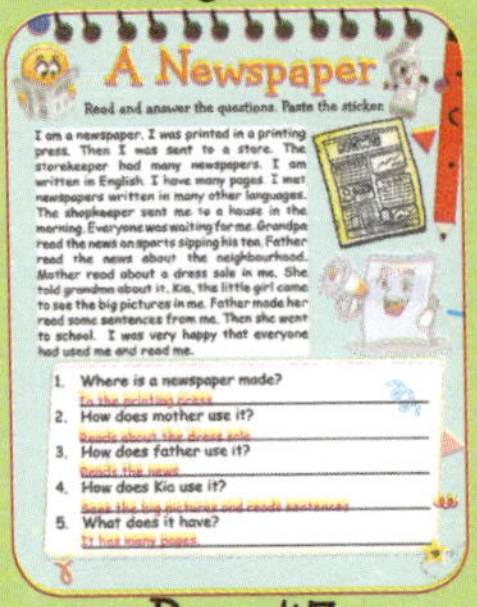
Page-47

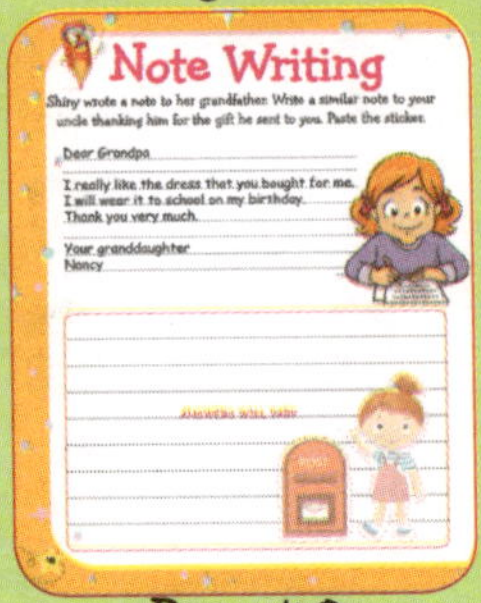
Page-48

Page-49

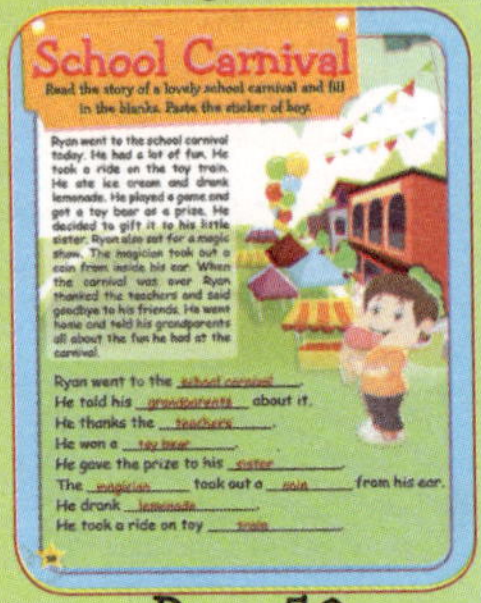
Page-50

Page-51

Page-52

Page-53

Page-54

Page-55

Page-56

Page-57

Page-58

Page-59

Page-60

Page-61

Page-62

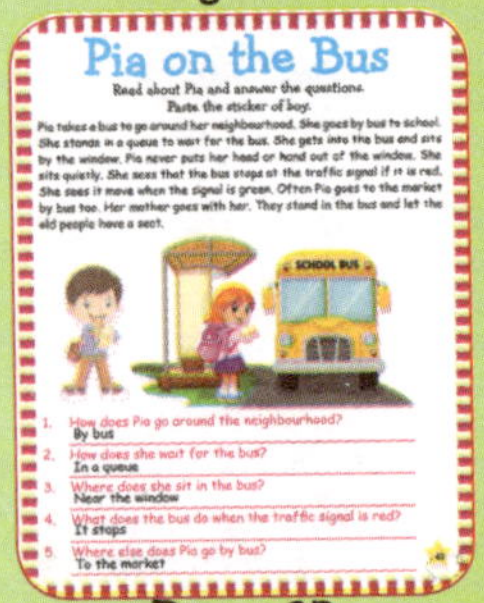
Page-63

Page-64

Page-65

Page-66

Page-67

Page-68

Page-69

Page-70

Pages 3-10

Pages 11-20

Pages 21-30

Pages 31-40

Pages 41-50

Pages 51-60

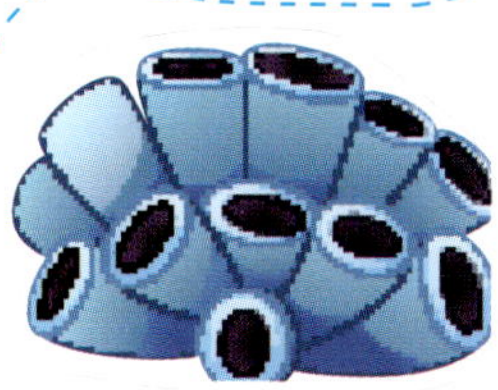

Pages 61-70